Love Journey

Living, Loving and Learning
Along the Way

by
Shantel Haskins

Watersprings
PUBLISHING

Published by Watersprings Publishing, a division of Watersprings Media House, LLC.
P.O. BOX 1284
Olive Branch, MS 38654
www.waterspringsmedia.com
Contact publisher for bulk orders and permission requests.

Printed in the United States of America.

Library of Congress Control Number: 2020917640
ISBN-13: 978-1-948877-59-6

Dedicated to Rodney, Renee, and Nakyia Haskins

Special Thanks– To my grandmother
Aneta "Jearl" Anderson

"God said He would take us on a LOVE JOURNEY"
–Aneta Anderson

A special thank you to my family, friends, and colleagues; for the kind and encouraging remarks over the years. Thank you to everyone that has ever provided a helping hand. I am thankful to be able to share my triumphs with people that have guided me, cared for me, and loved me continually. I am blessed to have such wonderful people in my life.

Choose to love
and let that
decision take
you on a journey.

Table of Contents

Love in Many Ways

Part 1

Traces of Your Past

Pieces

I was never afraid of losing you.

I never seen anything all the way through.

I made a habit out of leaving.

I was good at goodbye.

I wanted to protect myself, not noticing I was hurting someone else.

I loved hard but it was still easy for me to leave.

I loved the chase but enjoyed the release.

I craved attention but needed my freedom.

I wanted you, but I needed me more.

I never stayed to see what we could have been.

I enjoyed the flame but eventually, I put the fire out to watch the ash dance then miss the flame.

I would leave for every reason.

I was looking for someone that could give me a reason to stay.

I was the broken one. I became the people who shattered my heart.

I'm just pieces trying to love past my pain.

Wildfire

You are uncontrollable the essence of a wildfire.

You spread, but I did not run from the flames.

The flames were intriguing.

Something I wasn't supposed to be involved in.

I wanted to share your space.

Fire needs oxygen to live but suffocates the remainder of life.

I ignored the smoke and I wanted the flame.

I thought I was the only one that admired you.

I realized I was lost in you.

I was the house burning from you.

You didn't save me.

You let me burn slowly. I left and saved myself.

It took a while to heal from the damage you caused.

I no longer grieve in the ashes; I am the beauty that came from them.

Weakness

I was easily influenced; my actions always seemed to cater to your needs.

I loved you, that was my flaw.

I starved my talents in order to feed your desires.

You seduced my insecurities and it projected to the world.

I allowed you to be my weakness.

Doubt

I asked for an explanation and you gave me rambling
statements, fragments of deception.

I asked for your time, and all you could provide was an
excuse.

I asked you if you had been with someone else, you
reassured me that what we had was special.

I asked you were you hiding something, you said that I had
trust issues.

I asked if you loved me.

Before I let you answer, I walked away. I didn't have
the desire to hear the response anymore. I was more
disappointed in myself that I had to ask such a question. I
no longer relied on your shallow words, but your actions.

Love is kind

Love is the purest element found on this planet

Love is the connection of two souls

Love is a limitless boundary

Love is a multiple entity

Love is the greatest joy

Love is the biggest heartache

Love is the strongest hold you can have on somebody

Love is the core of your affection

Love is a vast infatuation

Love is accompanied by every emotion

To know that I have loved means that I can love again, for it is a journey

Part 2

Make a Choice

Lost in Lust

It wasn't the fact that I liked the way your lips felt on my skin,
it was the fact that I tasted deceit and chose to ignore it.
You touched my desire.
You attacked my vulnerability; it was no match for your
charm.
I felt time stopped when I was with you and every second
away from you, a battle against the minutes.
I wanted that feeling that I had when I was with you, sounds
that mimic an addict.
You were trouble in the midst of yearning for brighter days.
You were the storm I ignored and only knew your wrath once
I was entangled in you.
It took me a while to notice you only enjoyed the physical.
I'll now only seek love. I finally recognize the difference.

Presentation vs Expectation

I want to get lost in you and truly cater to your inner thoughts.

I want to be reminded why I was on a journey with you.

Every day in your smile, I want to see a glimpse of when our eyes first danced with each other.

Blind me from the hurt and have better days with me.

Lay with me and only want my mind if it's just for a moment.

What do you see in me?

Who do you refer to me as when I'm not around?

I want to know in the midst of your daydream what captured you when time stood still for you.

If I moved, would you follow?

Do you desire to cease forever with me?

Do you know how many tears have fallen from my eyes, with you being the cause?

Are you willing to let me walk alone?

Do you recognize how your actions affect me?

Do we share the same fears?

Do I carry unrealistic expectations...until I don't recognize what is being presented to me?

A Step Forward

You can't afford to look back.

That time has passed.

What is behind you is no more.

What is ahead is prosperity.

You cannot stand still and battle your past.

Your future deserves a fair chance with no limitations.

There is healing in momentum.

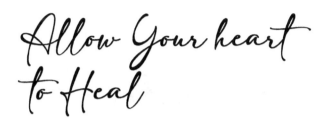

Allow Your heart to Heal

Some may say I broke up with you;

in reality I woke up from you.

I was in a haze of loving your potential.

What you presented was all you had to offer.

Traces of my past, gentle reminders of your touch cloud my
judgment.

I didn't know my heart was damaged until I was forced to
look at my pain in the mirror.

I had to choose not to dwell on the reflection.

I'm moving forward is what I remind myself. I don't know
if I'm convincing myself or my memories. Missing you is
apparent, but healing is progression.

Perspective

You look in my eyes, but I can tell you don't really see me.
I'm beyond what you think of me.
 I can't convince you on what parts of me to love.
If you saw me, you would love my triumphs and pick me up in my downfalls.
I can't force you to see what everyone around does.

Part 3

Love Patterns

Grace ____

It's okay that my heart has been broken;
for there is grace.
It's okay that I've failed at love;
for there is grace.
It's okay that I fell in love too fast;
for there is grace.
It's okay that I didn't notice what you needed from me;
for there is grace.
It's okay that I did not give you my all;
for there is grace.
We as people can be our own biggest critics.
Give yourself grace for your mistakes and fall in love
with the fact that you have a chance to get it right.

Forgiveness ___

I could not ignore hurt
and in time I forgave
I could not ignore disrespect
and in time I forgave
I could not ignore the lies
and in time I forgave
I could not ignore your deceptive patterns
and in time I forgave
I could not ignore your manipulation
and in time I forgave
I choose my liberation by forgiving your actions.

It Wasn't Picture Perfect

I reach out to you and you are not there
It's not all about life being fair
I let you walk away and pretend not to care
Now alone, only time to sit and stare
How does one function, so used to being a pair?
Pictures in a frame of us but I couldn't see past the glare.

Win the War_____

I can't go back and forth with you, I'm at war with your
emotions
I'm losing the battle with you
How can I expect you to stay and work it out, when all
you know how to do is argue and leave
Fight for me
Show up for us

Ex For a Reason

My ex only wanted two things out of life and I wasn't
one of them.
He loved the girl in me.
I was a woman.
He wanted to play games all day.
I wanted to write, win, and pray.
He couldn't be my rock.
He couldn't be consistent.
He couldn't be compassionate.
He couldn't be financially stable.
He couldn't be honest.
He couldn't be considerate.
He couldn't be kind.
He couldn't be loyal.

For all he couldn't be, I had to leave.

Part 4

Activate Love

Ride the Wave

I've never seen the depth of the ocean

I want to ride the waves to an unexplored region
I'll sail on a path as long as it leads to you

I want to lay in a sea of truth
I want to inhale anew
In order to do so my faith has to reach beyond the
shore

Thirst

I thirst for you
your touch,
your words,
your company.

When you are away
I crave you.
I suffer for you.

You are the water to my flowers
We are in a vase of desire.

I need you to quench my habits, and
starve
my loneliness.

Mind

Mind, I'm losing it's a terrible thing.

I'll blow your mind with my troubled past.
I'm trying to find someone who doesn't mind my flaws
but falls for more than my potential.

Do you mind loving me; you know trusting me.

Vows

To my Husband,

I've put my hands in your hands and on today I put my heart in your hands for now and forever more.

Today I bind my life with yours and our souls will tie together forever.

God has blessed this day far before now as we are entering into our destiny.

God molded me into the woman that stands before you and conditioned my heart to allow love to flow; in you I've found love, joy, and happiness and may I always be overwhelmed by this blessing.

My heart now beats with your rhythm.

You are my best friend. I commit my love, fidelity, and loyalty to you and only you as your wife.

Though hardships may surface let our LOVE be the anchor.

I've waited for you.

I enter into everyday with you and every moment with you.

Your fears, dreams, excitement, and tears are mine.

You dissolve any doubt and I know I am the woman for you, and you are the man for me.

May the declaration of my mind, heart, and logic align with God's will and our union in debt the sacrifices of Jesus dying on the cross, I LOVE YOU and always will.

To My Wife,

As you lay at night, and open your eyes to begin a new day, I just want to be there because in you I see life.

God has graced our paths to meet and in Him may our journey continue.

I am a better man because of you, I have seen hope where there once was not.

I have faith that I will protect you, provide for you, and care for you until the end of my days.

I respect your mind, body, spirit, and how your purpose will also
become mine.

When you smile my world is alright.
You are the Queen of my castle where my heart was engaged - you now hold the key.
I can be strong because I know you are with me and if ever we grow weak, may God and our LOVE lift us up.
You are my family.
I am now your husband. My strength is the reflection of your belief in me.
I vow these things to be true, I LOVE YOU.

Love journey

I thought once I said I love you, that was all I needed to do

I did not realize once I came to the destination of love I had to commit to loving you from that moment forward until you evolved into a new version of yourself.

I thought once I traveled to your heart that was all I needed to do.

I didn't realize you would change and adapt, as your environment changed.

I thought once I knew your favorite things, that was all I needed to do.

I didn't realize you would change over the years.

I didn't realize I was stuck loving the younger version of you...I have to let go of that so I can love you now...how you are and how you will be.

Let the destination take you on a Journey.

To anyone who has loved,

is in love,

or has yet

to love.

Share the Love!

If you use social media, please take a picture of or with Love Journey and be sure to mention **@Mendmybrokenpieces.** I would love to see where your journey has taken you.

About the Author

Shantel Haskins is a poet born and raised in Durham, NC. She was born to Rodney and Renee Haskins. Haskins has one sister, Nakyia Haskins. Haskins has a Bachelor of Arts degree in Political Science from Winston-Salem State University. Haskins also played collegiate softball while attending the University and has several athletic accomplishments.

In 2017, Haskins created Mend My Broken Pieces which is a platform that encourages artistic expression. Haskins created a website that would house her many poems of the same name. Mend My Broken Pieces which begin as a blog now invites community outreach engagements. Haskins is a poet exploring the limitless boundaries of the world and sharing her experiences through writing along the way.

Connect with Shantel:
Facebook/Instagram-
Mend My Broken Pieces /@mendmybrokenpieces
Website: www.mendmybrokenpieces.com

CPSIA information can be obtained
at www.ICGtesting.com
Printed in the USA
BVHW041724270721
612800BV00006BA/207

9 781948 877596